Cover photos courtesy of:
Climate Change: Stuart Miles at FreeDigitalPhotos.net
Pesticides: Suat Eman at FreeDigitalPhotos.net
GMOs: Vichaya Kiatying-Angsulee at FreeDigitalPhotos.net

To Carol, who endlessly supported the idea from the very first conversation to the very end. Thank you.

"We are the first generation to feel the sting of climate change and the last generation to be able to do anything about it."

Washington State Governor, Jay Inslee

Introduction

It's easy to say:
Climate change is too big a problem to solve, I'm only one person.
Or
It's too late, it's going to happen anyway, so what can I do about it?
Or
There is so much conflicting information out there, who should I believe?
Or
Buying fresh, local, and organic is expensive and time consuming.

I've heard them all many times, in fact, I've even said them myself in the past, but once you do that one thing, take that first step, then the next step just comes naturally.

Before you know it, you're asking the guy at the fish counter where those fish were caught and if they were they flash frozen, troll caught, or responsibly farmed.
Then you find yourself choosing not to buy the Chilean grapes due to the amount of carbon and energy it took to get those grapes from Chile to your grocery store.
You resolve to never (or almost never) buy water in plastic bottles, because you've seen photos of the miles-long, plastic-filled trash islands in the ocean.
You begin jotting down the dates and times of your local farmers markets so you can support local farmers and eat healthier.

Then, a miracle occurs: You notice all the "organic" and "non-GMO" labelling on products; you realize that all the little changes you've made are contributing to the changes that are occurring right now; and, you believe that one person can actually make a difference, and that person is you. ☺

Table of Contents

Earth
-Waste
-Pesticides
-Responsible Farming Practices
-Rising Temperatures, Droughts, and Floods

Here's What You Can Do...

Air
-CO2 Emissions
-Pesticides
-Birds, Bees and Butterflies
-Ozone Smog

Here's What You Can Do...

Food
-Organic Responsible Farming Practices
-Waste
-Malnutrition
- Preventable Diseases on the Rise
-Genetically Modified Food

Here's What You Can Do...

Water
-Climate Change and Melting Ice Sheets
-Sea Life
-Conservation
-Ocean Pollution

Here's What You Can Do...

Summary

Quick Reference Guide – Here's What You Can Do...

Additional Reading/Resources

Earth

Waste

Image courtesy of hinnamsaisuy at FreeDigitalPhosot.net

"Give a Hoot, Don't Pollute," said Woodsy Owl. That's the slogan I grew up with and it has stuck with me to this day. Unfortunately, not everyone got the message.

In his book *Outsmart Waste*, Tom Szacky begins: "Garbage is a uniquely human concept that does not exist in nature." He goes on to explain the circle of life, where fox droppings fertilize a berry bush that produces berries to feed a bird, that becomes the fox's dinner. This is not a pretty image for the bird, in the end, but this is how the planet has worked for millennia. Now add to the mix synthetics, plastics, and other non-biodegradable materials, and you have human waste—millions of tons per year to be exact—with no place to put it.

According to a *National Geographic* article by Dan Kulpinski, "Americans discard four-fifths of a ton of trash per person per year. Over half of that ends up in landfills, while a third is recycled and the rest goes to incinerators. In the past fifty years, solid waste has nearly tripled from 88.1 million tons per year to 249.9 million tons per year."

That is a lot of trash and that's every year, year after year, with no signs of slowing. Keep in mind that these numbers only represent the trash created in the United States. It's staggering.

Here's What You Can Do...

-Reduce the amount you throw away (including food waste).
-Re-use whatever you can.
-Re-cycle everything that is recyclable.
-Share with your friends and family interesting ways to reduce, re-use, and re-cycle.
-Do not buy water or any beverage in plastic bottles. Use refillables instead.
-Use re-usable containers for sandwiches and other lunch items.
-Compost food waste for your garden or create a worm garden.
-Only buy the fruits and vegetables that you need for the week ahead.
-Cut up the plastic rings that go around beverage 6-packs before you dispose of them.
-Do everything in your power to ensure that all plastics that you use are recycled when you are finished with them

Pesticides

Photo Courtesy of Sura Nualpradid at FreeDigitalPhotos.net

Pesticides are designed to kill, and they do.
Some pesticides are so dangerous that their effects on food and humans go on long after the pesticides have done their job. The trouble is, sadly, that they kill far more than they were designed to.

According to the Pesticide Action Network (PAN), the US EPA sets limits on the maximum amount of each pesticide that can be present on each food item, however, there is no limit to the number of different pesticides that can be on your food (and each pesticide then interacts with the others). In this way, pesticides can have a cumulative "toxic loading" effect, both in the immediate and long-term, with each person accumulating and responding to chemicals in a way that is biochemically and biographically unique. From birth, we build up a chemical "body burden" that reflects a combination of childhood and workplace exposures that includes pesticide residues on food, chemicals in our homes and personal care products, and the quality of air and water in our communities.

According to the Agency for Toxic Substances and Disease Registry (ATSDR), DDT was banned in the United States in 1972—more than forty years ago. However, because of its chemical characteristics, it has stayed in the environment and low levels may be present in fruits, vegetables, meat, and fish today. DDT has been linked to the near-extinction of the bald eagle, as well as the prevalence of many forms of cancer. Due to the banning of DDT, chemical companies have had to create new pesticides, and they have. But now there is a new threat to be concerned about: Neonicotinoids, or "neonics" for short. There are on-going studies in Canada, France, Mexico, and England linking neonics to dwindling bird, bee, insect, and marine life populations. This may prove devastating to our ecosystems.

Here's What You Can Do...

-Buy organic produce whenever you can.
-Eat organically grown meats and seafood.
-Go to www.panna.org and click on "What's in my Food?"
-Learn about pesticides and share what you know with family and friends.
-Stop using pesticides in and around your home.
-Look for restaurants in your area that support farm-to-table.

Responsible Farming Practices

Image Courtesy of amenic181 at FreeDigitalPhotos.net

According to Sustainabletable.org: "sustainable farms produce crops and raise animals without relying on toxic chemical pesticides, synthetic fertilizers, and genetically modified seeds or practices that degrade soil, water, or other resources. By growing a variety of plants and using techniques such as crop rotation, conservation tillage, and pasture-based livestock husbandry, sustainable farms protect biodiversity and foster the development and maintenance of healthy ecosystems."

That is quite a statement about the power of responsible farming practices, and many would and do dispute it.

At Worldwatch.org, "Can Organic Farming Feed Us All?" presents several studies that show that organic crop yields are comparable to conventional crop yields, both in developed and underdeveloped nations. The article states: "Contrary to critics who jibe that it's going back to farming like our grandfathers did, or that most of Africa already farms organically and it can't do the job, organic farming is a sophisticated combination of old wisdom and modern ecological innovations that help harness the yield-boosting effects of nutrient cycles beneficial to insects and crop synergies. It's heavily dependent on technology—just not the technology that comes out of a chemical plant."

It's well past time to marry the old and the new and farm right, instead of relying on the trial and error method we've been subjected to for the past century or so. We do not need GMO foods to feed everyone, nor do we need to kill off every insect we consider to be a pest to our crops with harsh chemicals that we don't know the long term effects of (which leads to harming and killing off innocent bystanders that happen along at the wrong time, too).

Here's What You Can Do...

-Buy organic foods as much as possible.
-Buy fresh, local, and organic from your local farmers market.
-Talk to your grocer and insist on local, organic, non GMO food choices.
-Buy products labeled "organic" and "non-GMO."
-Ask where your fresh produce -i.e those grapes and cucumbers, are coming from.
-Shop seasonally and enjoy local fresh produce

Rising Temperatures, Droughts, and Floods

Image Courtesy of coward_lion at FreeDigitalPhotos.net

I don't think it's a surprise to anyone that the hots are getting hotter and the colds are getting colder. Storms are more intense and are occurring with greater frequency. Could this be part of the natural weather patterns of the planet? Maybe, but many studies indicate that human activities are a contributing factor, at the very least. So, perhaps it's time for a change in human activities.

"Global Warming" was the early name for what we now call Climate Change, and whether you believe in it or not, these changes are taking place around the world.

I recently heard a politician commenting on "global warming," indicating that he didn't believe in it since he had just survived one of the coldest winters on record. That's the kind of thinking that contributes to the divide between the skeptics and the rest of us.

On the National Wildlife Federation site, in an article titled "Global Warming and Extreme Weather," we learn that "this intensification of weather and climate extremes will be the most visible impact of global warming in our everyday lives. It is also causing dangerous changes to the landscape of our world, adding stress to wildlife species and their habitat."

Make no mistake, planet Earth will continue doing what it has always done, with or without us. What matters is what humans do in the next several decades that will help determine which path the planet takes.

Here's What You Can Do...

-Reduce your carbon footprint http://cotap.org/reduce-carbon-footprint/
-Drive less by consolidating your errands and working from home one day per week.
-Eat less meat and implement a no-meat day once a week in your home.
-Reduce waste from your home and re-cycle everything you possibly can.
-Waste less food so that it doesn't end up in landfills.

CO2 Emissions

Image Courtesy of njaj at FreeDigitalPhotos.net

In May of 2013, *National Geographic* magazine published an article stating that the amount of carbon dioxide in the air had exceeded 400 ppm (parts per million), for the first time in the fifty- five years we have been measuring it—and probably more than three million years of Earth's history. To be clear, CO2 levels peak every year in May, but begin falling as spring arrives and plants begin to bloom and breathe and clean the air for us.

The *National Geographic* article goes on to say: "Scientists have warned that CO2 levels above 450 ppm could result in dangerous disruptions of the climate. Some think that we may have already passed the danger threshold."

Passing the 400 ppm mark is a big deal, and is likely to become standard on a regular basis, given humanity's current lifestyle choices.

It's important to remember that reducing the CO_2 emissions is only half of the equation to maintaining cleaner air. We must also be sure that there is enough vegetation to help clean the air for us; so, rather than de-foresting the planet, it is in our best interest as a species to re-forest it.

Here's What You Can Do...

-Plant a tree on your birthday and teach your kids to do the same. Trees help to clean the air of toxins.
-Buy recycled paper products whenever you can.
-Check with your local energy supplier to see if they offer wind or solar.
-Reduce your reliance on gas and oil where possible.
-Walk, bike, and use public transit when you can.
-Reduce the amount of beef you eat, but when you do, make sure it's local grass fed beef.

Pesticides

Photo Courtesy of Toa55 at FreeDigitalPhotos.net

It's no surprise that many pesticides are airborne, so that deep breath you take on a crisp clear morning may very well be carrying airborne pesticide particulates. This is thanks to something called pesticide drift, which occurs when pesticides unintentionally move away from the application site. In simpler terms, when the wind carries pesticides away from the intended pests and delivers them into the air we breathe, it drops them in our rivers and streams and onto plants and food we eat.

According to the National Pesticide Information Center (NPIC), air quality is a measure of the amount of pollutants in our atmosphere, which includes indoor and outdoor air. The Air Quality Index (AQI) tells you how clean or polluted the air you are breathing is, and outlines the health effects you may be subject to by breathing air that is polluted—not just in the short-term, but sometimes for days after exposure to air of poor quality.

The Air Quality Index is often reported on the news during the summer, when pollution tends to stagnate over populated areas, sometimes for days. The very young, the elderly, and those with pulmonary conditions are at the greatest risk for breathing polluted air.

Here's What You Can Do...

-Make your home, lawn, and garden pesticide-free.
- Practice IPM (Integrated Pest Management) by following instructions and guidelines at npic.orst.edu.
-Prevent pesticide drift by using products that break down quickly.
-If you must spray pesticides, don't spray them on a windy day.
-Avoid using airborne products whenever possible.

Birds, Bees, and Butterflies

Photo Courtesy of SweetCrisis at FreeDigitalPhotos.net

I mentioned earlier that DDT nearly wiped out the bald eagle population by being a contributing factor in the destruction of their food source. And while DDT poisoning was only one threat, it is important that we not make similar mistakes with the food chain going forward; we have to recognize the signs of species' decline and extinction before it's too late.

Currently our birds, bees, and butterflies are at risk. These populations are declining at rapid rates, which means trouble for our food supply chain.

I read recently on parksandrecreation.org that our children may not see a monarch butterfly in the wild. Can you imagine that?
I read too that one out of every three bites of food we eat is dependent on bees pollinating plants—but our pollinators are dying off due to Colony Collapse Disorder. There are several contributing factors to this collapse, but two important ones are mono-culture farming (which offers bees nothing to pollinate and no food source) and pesticides (including the new class of insecticides I mentioned earlier called neonicotinoids, or neonics).

When bees pollinate flowering plants that have been sprayed with insecticides and pesticides, they die. Because bees plays such a vital role in our food supply chain, it is in our best interest to keep them alive and healthy and pollinating. Swift and immediate attention is needed to address the bee population.

Pollinators give us our food. Just imagine going to your local grocery store or farmers market only to find that one-third of the produce you want is simply not there. If Colony Collapse Disorder and similar issues aren't corrected soon, we can expect to find even fewer of the foods we want—and need—in the future.

Here's What You Can Do...

-Start your own bee hive.

-Buy organic, pesticide-free produce.

-Buy local, from farmers and farmers markets.

-Never use spray pesticides in your garden.

-Talk to your city planners about planting wildflowers in public areas.

- Talk to your city planners about what they are spraying in and around your neighborhoods and schools.

Ozone Smog

Photo Courtesy of worradmu at FreeDigitialPhotos.net

According to the Natural Resources Defense Council, ozone smog forms when pollution from vehicles, factories, and other sources reacts with sunlight and heat. Increasing temperatures associated with climate change speed this process, and result in more smog. Added to the mix are ragweed and other allergens, which are expected to multiply and worsen as rising carbon dioxide levels cause plants to produce more pollen. Also, as dry areas become drier and we experience more drought and wildfires, smoke from burning landscapes intensifies poor air quality.

I'm not sure when the news started reporting pollution indexes, but I do know that the number of "bad air days" is on the rise, along with the number of people who suffer from asthma and allergies. Clean air is a necessity for all of us, but for those who have asthma, allergies, and COPD—as well as the very young and the elderly—the lack of clean air could be life threatening. One of the most alarming parts of this clean air "crisis," is that only eleven states are currently addressing the issue.

Here's What You Can Do...

-Drive less, even 1 day per week less can make a big difference.

-Find out what your state is doing to address air quality.

-Recognize "bad air days" and limit outdoor activities on such days.

-Use public transit if you can.

-Consider riding a bike or carpooling to work if you can

-When you drive, drive with purpose by combining multiple trips into one.

Food

Organic, Responsible Farming Practices

Photo courtesy of Stuart Miles at FreeDigitalPhotos.net

I've already addressed organic farming, so here I'll address mono-cropping, the practice I brought up as a problem for bees. Mono-cropping utilizes a very large area of land for only one crop, year after year after year. Now, anyone who has ever had a garden knows the importance of planting a variety of flowers, fruits, or vegetables. Doing so keeps your soil nutrient-rich, and when carefully planned, improves your garden's output into future growing seasons. Blow this personal garden concept up 100 or 1000 times, and you can see how it makes perfect sense to do the same thing with large-scale or industrial farming.

According to *sustainabletable.org*, "mono-cropping causes crop vulnerability to insects, weeds, fungi and other pests... this vulnerability often requires intensive use of insecticides, fungicides and/or herbicides."

So, the practice of mono-cropping not only depletes the soil of nutrients, which will result in lower crop yields, but also causes insects and pests to multiply, which in turn requires intensive use of chemicals. We already know how chemicals negatively affect other species in the food chain, so the question is: Why continue the practice of mono-cropping?

Here's What You Can Do...
   -Buy from local farms who practice crop rotation.
   -Buy from local farmers at farmers markets and ask about their farming practices (farmers love to talk about farming).
   -Move your food dollars from agro-industry to local farmers.
   -Change your retirement investments from chemical companies to sustainable green companies.

Food Waste

Photo courtesy of blogs.plos.org

In an article at NRDC.Org (Natural Resource Defense Council), entitled: How America is Losing up to 40% of its Food from Farm to Fork to Landfill", author Dana Gunders states "Getting food from the farm to our fork eats up 10% of the total US energy budget, uses 50% of US land, and swallows 80% of all freshwater consumed in the United States. Yet 40% of food in the US today goes uneaten". At a time when 1 in 7 people are struggling with hunger, these numbers are astonishing.
She further states that Americans are throwing out the equivalent of $165 billion each year.

Of that number, says takepart.com, $750 million is spent just to dispose of the food we carelessly toss in the trash. So we not only waste tons of food, we then spend millions to dispose of it. It makes no sense.

Here's one more fact that might get your attention: Food waste that goes to the landfill breaks down anaerobically and produces methane—a gas that is twenty-one times more potent than CO_2 as a greenhouse gas. Oh my!

So, it's one thing to buy fresh and local and to avoid pesticides and GMOs, but if a huge portion of what we buy goes into the trash, then we're only getting it half right.

Here's What You Can Do…

-Be aware of what you buy, plan menus, and buy only what you will use for the week.
-Be aware of what you throw away – could it be leftovers? Could it go into a soup or stew?
-Don't worry about buying the "perfect" fruits and vegetables at the grocery store. Misshapen produce is still edible, and bruises can be cut out.
-Create an "eat me first" shelf in your fridge, and eat the oldest food first to avoid throwing it away.
-Read "best buy" date information, and understand that food and beverages are not bad after that date, they are just not at peak freshness.

Malnutrition

Photo Courtesy of David Castillo Dominici at FreeDigitalPhotos.net

It seems odd that one of the wealthiest countries in the world, the United States, could have a malnutrition problem—but we do. Right here in the US, approximately 1% of children suffer from chronic malnutrition.

What does malnutrition even mean? Simply put, it is bad or poor nutrition. Malnutrition occurs in people who are either undernourished or over nourished. Undernutrition occurs when not enough essential nutrients are consumed; overnutrition occurs when people eat too much, eat the wrong things, don't exercise, or take too many vitamins or other dietary replacements (yes, that's possible).

The Worldwatch Institute states that for the first time in human history the number of overweight people rivals the number of underweight people. While the world's underfed population has declined slightly since 1980 to 1.1 billion, the number of overweight people has surged to 1.1 billion.

In a Worldwatch paper titled "Underfed and Overfed," Gary Gardner states that the public health impact of malnutrition is enormous: More than half of the world's disease burden—measured in years of healthy life lost—is attributable to hunger, overeating, and widespread vitamin and mineral deficiencies. The century with the greatest potential to eliminate malnutrition instead, has seen it boosted to record levels.

Food Afterthought: the beauty industry – haircare and cosmetics – is a billion dollar industry. I am oftentimes astonished at what we will spend on our external appearance while, at the same time, complaining about the cost of high quality, Non GMO, organic food. It seems to me that we should all, at a minimum, spend as much on what goes inside our precious organs as we spend on our hair and face. After all, proper nutrition will definitely affect the hair and skin anyway, so if you spend more on what goes inside you may get to spend less on what goes on outside.

Here's What You Can Do…

-Use food as fuel and nutrition for your body
-Choose the right kind of foods, rich in nutrients
-Read labels and avoid ingredients that you can't pronounce
- Work with your doctor or nutritionist to find what works for you
-Replace poor food choices with whole, fresh, organic food
-Keep a food diary and notice what you putting inside your body, organs and bloodstream
- Read labels and discover the hidden sugars in so called "healthy" products.

Preventable Diseases on the Rise

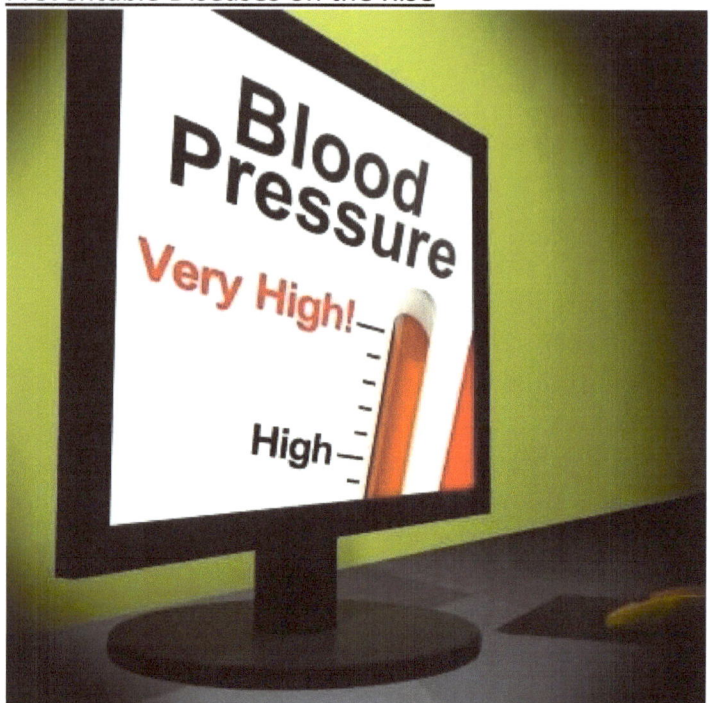

Photo Courtesy of Stuart Miles at FreeDigitalPhotos.net

The percentage of overweight people has expanded rapidly in recent decades, so much so that it has offset any health system gains which might have resulted from a modest decline in hunger statistics. In the United States, 55% of adults are overweight, and one in five American children are now classified as overweight too.

Sadly, the same trends are occurring in developing nations as well. Internationally, 23% of adults are considered obese. Co-author of *Underfed and Overfed*, Brian Halwell, states that many nations have simply traded hunger for obesity, and diseases of poverty for diseases of excess.

Type 2 diabetes, heart disease and stroke, high blood pressure, cancer, gallbladder disease, osteoarthritis, gout and sleep apnea—all these health risks are linked to obesity, according to WebMD. The saddest truth of all? Obesity is a preventable disease.

According to the Center for Disease Control (CDC), the medical costs for people who are obese are $1,429 per year higher than for those of normal weight. But is doesn't stop there. The Fair Food Network cites a study conducted by the Get America Fit Foundation that says medical care to treat obesity-related diseases and to make up for lower work productivity and higher work absenteeism, costs US companies $45 billion per year. Clearly, obesity and its ill effects are a problem for everyone—one way or another, everyone ends up paying—not just those who are obese.

Here's What You Can Do...

-If you are obese, and it is a result of overeating, work with your doctor to determine a healthy weight and develop a plan to get there. Don't give up if you have a setback: the results will be worth the effort.
-Move a little more every day, it all counts.
-Eat fresh, local, and organic whenever you can.
-Look for healthy meal replacements.
-Eat a rainbow by developing a love of colorful fresh foods.

Genetically Modified Foods

Photo Courtesy of Vichaya Kiatying-Angsulee at FreeDigitalPhotos.net

From the many articles I've read about Genetically Modified Foods (or, GMOs, which stands for Genetically Modified Organisms), no idea has surprised me more than the idea that GMOs were initially intended to increase crop yields and to lengthen shelf life, in order to meet the food needs of a growing population. The GMO movement began as a worthy cause, indeed, but instead, has led to unintended consequences which include "superbugs" that are immune to pesticides, which in turn has resulted in the creation of newer, stronger pesticides. Additionally, the rise in food allergies has been attributed to GMOs, and multiple studies link GMOs to kidney damage, liver damage, and other health issues.

From PBS.org, Jeremy Rifkin notes that when you introduce a GMO into the environment, you have to remember that it is alive and unpredictable. GMOs can reproduce, mutate, migrate, and proliferate over wide regions. No, this isn't some contained lab experiment: genetically modified organisms are out there, blowing in the wind, re-creating, and becoming part of the "new" nature. What's even scarier is that the full effects of introducing GMOs into our world are only just beginning to reveal themselves. The full story is far from over, and more is being discovered and written every day.

The Institute for Responsible Technology notes that before the FDA decided to allow GMOs into food without labelling, FDA scientists had repeatedly warned that GM foods can create unpredictable, hard to detect toxins and side effects, including allergies, new diseases, and nutritional problems. For many years, these scientists have urged long-term safety studies, but have been ignored. Again, the story on GMOs is still be written, but the ending does not look good.

Here's What You Can Do...
>   -Look for Non GMO labelling on foods you buy and eat
>   -Watch Genetic Roulette: http://geneticroulettemovie.com/ and share with everyone you know
>   -Know the fab 14 and terrible 20 when you shop: https://www.caltonnutrition.com/rich-food/wallet-guide/
>   -Look for foods that are certified USDA Organic or Non GMO project verified
>   -Avoid all corn, soy and canola (highest GMO crops) that are not specifically labelled Non GMO
>   -Your produce label number will begin with a 9 if it is organic

Water

Climate Change – Melting Ice Sheets

Photo Courtesy of Federico Stevanin at FreeDigitalPhotos.net

According to NASA, the collapse of the West Antarctic Ice Sheet is unstoppable. Sea level will rise close to three feet by the year 2100.

Depending on what study you read, those projections could accelerate, depending on what factors take place in the coming years. I recently saw a graphic showing two Texas sized chunks having already been lost .
http://www.bing.com/images/search?q=arctic+sea+loss+size+of+2+texas&view=detailv2&qpvt=arctic+sea+loss+size+of+2+texas&id=CB574BB8854EE0AB7D6EBFB489D1939C80FD453F&selectedIndex=28&ccid=JYfXNfRo&simid=608007343984611019&thid=OIP.M2587d735f468aaccfcdba059f703ff2co0&ajaxhist=0

Additionally, something called ocean acidification is rising and spreading around the globe. The World Wildlife Federation (WWF) states that the global ocean is 25% more acidic than it was three hundred years ago, a change that is traceable to increasing levels of atmospheric CO_2. Further acidification is a threat to subarctic fisheries, including those in the Bering Sea, and entails major socioeconomic consequences.

According to Larry Hinzman and Dr. John Walsh, members of Global Change Connection to the Arctic (GCCA,) "mitigation activities such as reduced emission have the potential to alter the trajectory of Arctic Climate Change in the latter decades of the present century. However, some changes are already "locked" in the evolving climate system, making adaptation a crucial element for dealing with climate change over the next few decades. Furthermore, despite increasing awareness of the importance of making climate change adaptations as soon as possible, in the US Arctic (Alaska) and other Arctic regions, environmental and climate policies have, to date, been dominated by planning and monitoring, rather than implementation".

So there's the rub right? We were hasty, nay, aggressive in our efforts to increase production of things, energy, and food; and now, when it's time to act to make corrections, we are reluctant to make a move. There's no profit in cleaning up the mess we've made, only survival.

Here's What You Can Do...
-Help reduce CO_2 emissions, this cannot be overstated.
-Buy and throw away less stuff, specially plastics that you know will end up in a landfill.
-Use less energy whenever possible - In your home, unplug appliances when not in use.
-Drive less, consolidate trips before running errands. Ask people in the house if they need you to pick up anything for them.

-Walk, ride a bike, use mass transit if you can.

-Buy an electric or hybrid car.

- Consume less beef by implementing a no meat Monday practice.

Sea Life

Photo Courtesy of think4photop at FreeDigitalPhotos.net

By now most everyone is aware of the plight of the polar bears. The melting ice sheets are reducing the size of their habitat and the spring is arriving earlier, resulting in less hunting time for them. But there are many other varieties of sea life being affected as well.

The sea lions are having a hard time finding a place to bask in the sun, mate, and give birth to their pups. The fish they eat are going farther out into the ocean in search of colder water. The sea lions are starving or changing their diet, resulting in lower nutrition for themselves and their babies.

According to the World Wildlife Federation (WWF), a condition called coral bleaching is spreading around the world with coral mortality reaching 70% in some regions. Additionally, the WWF states that marine species affected by climate change include plankton, which forms the basis for marine food chains consisting of coral, fish, polar bears, walruses, seals, sea lions, penguins, and sea birds.

They go on to state that rising temperatures can directly affect the metabolism, life cycle, and behavior of marine species. For many species, temperature serves as a cue for reproduction. Clearly, changes in sea temperature could affect their successful breeding. The number of male and female offspring is determined by temperature for marine turtles, as well as some fish and copepods (tiny shrimp-like animals on which many other marine animals feed). Changing climate could therefore skew sex ratios and threaten population survival.

Here's What You Can Do...

-Reduce your carbon footprint (noticing a theme yet?), by reducing your reliance on gas and oil by driving one day less a week and limiting the plastics you use and dispose of.
-Eat and buy sustainable sea food species and ask your local restaurants if the seafood they're serving is sustainably raised, meaning that it is either caught or farmed in ways that consider the long-term vitality of harvested species and the well-being of the oceans.
-Enjoy the ocean in a responsible manner: Give a hoot, don't pollute. Be sure that all of the plastic that you take to the beach comes home with you.
-When on vacation, be respectful of the native ecosystem and do no harm.
-.

Water Conservation

Photo Courtesy of Stuart Miles at FreeDigitalPhotos.net

Did you know that washing your sidewalk or driveway with a hose uses fifty gallons of water… every five minutes!. Try using a broom instead.

Did you also know that three-fourths of water used indoors is used in the bathroom? We can all take shorter showers if we really try and we can turn off the water while we're brushing our teeth instead of letting it run. Same goes for when we are shaving: we could rinse our razors in standing water instead of running water.

According to EarthEasy.com, most people in North America use fifty to seventy gallons of indoor water each day, and about the same amount outdoors, depending on the season.

More than 50% of the world's fresh water comes from mountain runoff and snowmelt, according to the Grace Communications Foundation. As the Earth's temperature continues to rise, we can expect a significant impact on our fresh water supplies with the potential for devastating effects on these resources.

To help in this battle, the Grace Communications Foundation will identify your water footprint, determining the amount of water you use every day, which includes many measurements that may surprise you—like the amount of water it takes to produce all of the items you consume each day. It all counts. For more information on your water footprint go to gracelinks.org.

What You Can Do...
- Take shorter showers
- Turn the water off when brushing your teeth
- Only do laundry when you have a full load
- Find out what your water footprint is at www.gracelinks.org
- Never think of water as an endless resource

Ocean Pollution

Photo Courtesy of Artur84 at FreeDigitalPhotos.net

Have you ever heard of the Great Pacific garbage patch? If not, this is something you absolutely have to Google. You will be horrified by what we, as a species of consumers, have created. In 2014, NBC news reported that the garbage patch in the Pacific Ocean had grown to an expanse of hundreds of miles. The biggest patch is twice the size of Texas.

Let that sink in for a moment: A garbage patch twice the size of Texas is floating around the Pacific Ocean. And that's only one patch, there are more... there is one in every ocean.

According to Ocean Health Index:
http://www.oceanhealthindex.org/news/Death_By_Plastic
"Plastic Entanglements Increase 40% for Marine Animals"
To look at the photos of a badly deformed turtle who somehow managed to swim through a milk carton ring when he was a baby and then grew to adulthood with it still wrapped around his middle is so sad. Then there is the dead seal with a band of plastic wrapped around his nose and mouth, and the decaying body of a seagull with several plastic objects in his stomach. I could go on, but

you probably have come across a few of these visuals by now. Sorry about that, but between photos of dead or deformed animals and the ones of the hundreds of miles of trash floating around our oceans, if you aren't turned off of plastic at this point, then probably nothing will change your mind. When I think, or know really, that some of my trash has likely contributed to the death of these poor innocent creatures that don't even know what plastic is has definitely changed the way I look at all plastic.

Here's What You Can Do…
-Use no plastic if possible, or less plastic whenever you can.
-If you must use plastic, please use it responsibly re-use and recycle everything!
-Remember that the plastic you discard may be out of your sight, but it will never leave the planet.
-Stop buying water or any beverage in plastic bottles; use refillables instead.
-If you must buy plastic and it's possible that the parts you discard may harm an animal, please cut it in a way that will ensure it will not wrap around its neck or body.

Here' What You Can Do...
Summary...

Waste

-Reduce the amount you throw away (including food waste).
-Re-use whatever you can.
-Re-cycle everything that is recyclable.
-Share with your friends and family interesting ways to reduce, re-use, and re-cycle.
-Do not buy water or any beverage in plastic bottles. Use refillables instead.
-Use re-usable containers for sandwiches and other lunch items.
-Compost food waste for your garden or create a worm garden.
-Only buy the fruits and vegetables that you need for the week ahead.
-Cut up the plastic rings that go around beverage 6-packs before you dispose of them.
-Do everything in your power to ensure that all plastics that you use are recycled when you are finished with them

Pesticides

-Buy organic produce whenever you can.
-Eat organically grown meats and seafood.
-Go to www.panna.org and click on "What's in my Food?"
-Learn about pesticides and share what you know with family and friends.
-Stop using pesticides in and around your home.
-Look for restaurants in your area that support farm-to-table.

Responsible Farming Practices

-Buy organic foods as much as possible.
-Buy fresh, local, and organic from your local farmer's market.

-Talk to your grocer and insist on local, organic, non GMO food choices.
-Buy products labeled "organic" and "non-GMO."
-Ask where your fresh produce -i.e those grapes and cucumbers are coming from.
-Shop seasonally and enjoy local fresh produce

Rising Temperatures, Droughts and Floods
-Reduce your carbon footprint http://cotap.org/reduce-carbon-footprint/
-Drive less by consolidating your errands and working from home one day per week.
-Eat less meat and implement a no-meat day once a week in your home.
-Reduce waste from your home and re-cycle everything you possibly can.
-Waste less food so that it doesn't end up in landfills.

C02 Emissions
-Plant a tree on your birthday and teach your kids to do the same. Trees help to clean the air of toxins.
-Buy recycled paper products whenever you can.
-Check with your local energy supplier to see if they offer wind or solar.
-Reduce your reliance on gas and oil where possible.
-Walk, bike, and use public transit when you can.
-Reduce the amount of beef you eat, but when you do, make sure it's local grass fed beef.

Pesticides
-Make your home, lawn, and garden pesticide-free.
- Practice IPM (Integrated Pest Management) by following instructions and guidelines at npic.orst.edu.
-Prevent pesticide drift by using products that break down quickly.

-If you must spray pesticides, don't spray them on a windy day.
-Avoid using airborne products whenever possible.

Birds, Bees and Butterflies
-Start your own bee hive.
-Buy organic, pesticide-free produce.
-Buy local, from farmers and farmers markets.
-Never use spray pesticides in your garden.
-Talk to your city planners about planting wildflowers in public areas.
- Talk to your city planners about what they are spraying in and around your neighborhoods and schools.

Ozone Smog
-Drive less, even 1 day per week less can make a big difference.
-Find out what your state is doing to address air quality.
-Recognize "bad air days" and limit outdoor activities on such days.
-Use public transit if you can.
-Consider riding a bike or carpooling to work if you can
-When you drive, drive with purpose by combining multiple trips into one.

Organic Responsible Farming Practices
-Buy from local farms who practice crop rotation
-Buy from local farmers at farmer's markets and ask about their farming practices (farmers love to talk about farming)
-Move your food dollars from agro industry to local farmers
- Change your retirement investments from chemical companies to smaller green farmer

Food

-Be aware of what you buy, plan menus and buy only what you will use for the week.
-Be aware of what you throw away – could it be leftovers? Could it go into a soup or stew?
-Don't worry about buying the "perfect" fruits and vegetables at the grocery store. misshapen is still edible, and bruises can be cut out.
-Create am "eat me first" in your fridge and eat the oldest food first to avoid throwing it away.
-Read about the "best by" date information and understand that the food or beverage is not bad after that date, just not at its peak freshness.

Malnutrition

-Use food as fuel and nutrition for your body
-Choose the right kind of foods, rich in nutrients
-Read labels and avoid ingredients that you can't pronounce
- Work with your doctor or nutritionist to find what works for you
-Replace poor food choices with whole, fresh, organic food
-Keep a food diary and notice what you putting inside your body, organs and bloodstream
- Read labels and discover the hidden sugars in so called "healthy" products.

Preventable Diseases on the Rise

-If you are obese, and it is the result of overeating, work with your doctor to determine a healthy weight and develop a plan to get there, don't give up if you have a setback, the results are worth the effort
-Move a little more every day, it all counts
-Eat fresh, local and organic whenever you can
-Look for healthy meal replacements
- Eat a rainbow by developing a love of colorful fresh foods

Genetically Modified Foods

-Look for Non GMO labelling on foods you buy and eat
-Watch Genetic Roulette: http://geneticroulettemovie.com/
and share with everyone you know
-Know the fab 14 and terrible 20 when you shop:
https://www.caltonnutrition.com/rich-food/wallet-guide/
-Look for foods that are certified USDA Organic or Non GMO
project verified
-Avoid all corn, soy and canola (highest GMO crops) that are
not specifically labelled Non GMO
-Your produce label number will begin with a 9 if it is organic

Climate Change – Melting Ice Sheets
-Help reduce CO2 emissions, this cannot be overstated.
-Buy and throw away less stuff, specially plastics that you
know will end up in a landfill.
-Use less energy whenever possible - In your home, unplug
appliances when not in use.
-Drive less, consolidate trips before running errands. Ask
people in the house if they need you to pick up anything for
them.
-Walk, ride a bike, use mass transit if you can.
-Buy an electric or hybrid car.
- Consume less beef by implementing a no meat Monday
practice.

Sea Life

-Reduce your carbon footprint (noticing a theme yet?), by reducing your reliance on gas and oil by driving one day less a week and limiting the plastics you use and dispose of.

-Eat and buy sustainable sea food species and ask your local restaurants if the seafood they're serving is sustainably raised, meaning that it is either caught or farmed in ways that consider the long-term vitality of harvested species and the well-being of the oceans.

-Enjoy the ocean in a responsible manner: Give a hoot, don't pollute. Be sure that all of the plastic that you take to the beach comes home with you.

-When on vacation, be respectful of the native ecosystem and do no harm.

Conservation

-Take shorter showers

-Turn the water off when brushing your teeth

-Only do laundry when you have a full load

-Find out what your water footprint is at www.gracelinks.org

-Never think of water as an endless resource

Ocean Pollution

-Use no plastic if possible, or less plastic whenever you can.

-If you must use plastic, please use it responsibly re-use and recycle everything!

-Remember that the plastic you discard may be out of your sight, but it will never leave the planet.

-Stop buying water or any beverage in plastic bottles; use refillables instead.

-If you must buy plastic and it's possible that the parts you discard may harm an animal, please cut it in a way that will ensure it will not wrap around its neck or body.

Summary

There are no original ideas in this book. I have shamelessly collected amazing facts, quotes, and ideas from amazing people and thought leaders. I am presenting them here to you with the hope that something inside you will go off and you will say "Yes! Here is what I can do," and that you will actually take one or two steps as soon as possible, to make the changes we so desperately need to make— Today.

As a people, we can affect change. We have done it before:

1. When London was basting in pollution during the industrial revolution and people were dying, changes had to be made for their survival.
2. In the United States, when we realized that slavery was an archaic notion, changes were made to unify the country.
3. When it was time to enact equal rights for women, changes had to be made through laws within the government that gave women the right to vote in 1920.
4. When Wall Street crashed in 2008 and our economic way of life was at risk, changes had to be made to the way financial institutions were monitored and governed to turn our economy around.

Change is never quick or easy and there are always groups on both sides of every situation and issue, but when change is needed, it is we the people who have to bring it about.

We know that our governments—local, national, and global—are busy pushing their own agendas and making tiny incremental changes in the "right direction," while at the same time, funding polluters in the opposite direction.

If we are waiting for our governments to save us, we will be disappointed.

It is up to us as consumers, voters, entrepreneurs, and parents, to take action and make the changes we know are necessary to ensure our continued survival. The time is now! We can vote with our dollars and buy the right products; we can also stop buying so much of everything without any regard for where it will end up when we're finished with it.

When you think about it historically, isn't it our responsibility to help reverse the tide on this? Isn't a lot of the mess we're in, at least in part, our fault? Didn't we rapidly get used to all the modern conveniences, only to then want *more*? Didn't we learn to love stuff, regardless of whether we needed it or not?

We want it, we buy it, and we dispose of it. We've become over-buyers, over-eaters, and over-wasters, with no regard for what it takes to produce all of this excess, or what happens to it once we have finished with it. One little water bottle takes three times as much water to produce as is contained inside the bottle, and takes hundreds of years to decompose. Just one water bottling plant creates 1.5 million bottles a day. Do the math.

Enough!

My final disclaimer:

Do I follow all of my "Here's What You Can Do…" lists every day?

Of course not, but I check off as many items as I can, as often as I can, and I know with every ounce of my being that I'm making a difference.

My hope is that everyone reading this will do that *one thing, just one*—start today and see where tomorrow leads you.

Additional Reading/Research

Naomi Klein – *This Changes Everything*
Rachel Carson – *Silent Spring* (written 50 years ago)
Tom Szaky – *Outsmart Waste*
Jeffrey Smith – *Seeds of Deception* (book) and *Genetic Roulette*
(film) http://geneticroulettemovie.com/
Steve Druker – *Altered Genes*

YouTube

David Putnam – "The Reality of Climate Change"

Websites

Climate Institute – climate.org
World Wildlife Federation – Panda.org
National Organic Program – AMS.USDA.gov
Environmental Protection Agency – epa.gov/climatechange
Pesticide Action Network – panna.org
Agency for Toxic Substances and Disease Registry – atsdr.cdc.gov
Sustainable Table – sustainabletable.org
Worldwatch Institute – worldwatch.org
National Wildlife Federation – nwf.org
British Beekeepers Association – BBKA.org.uk
National Resource Defense Council – nrdc.org
Johns Hopkins Children's – hopkinschildren.org
Centers for Disease Control – cdc.gov
Institute for Responsible Technology – responsibletechnology.org
Earth Easy – eartheasy.com
Grace Communications Foundation – gracelinks.org
Takepart.com
Endfoodwastenow.org

Ted Talks

http://www.ted.com/topics/climate+change Climate Change
http://www.ted.com/search?q=GMO GMO's
https://www.ted.com/talks/shimon_steinberg_natural_pest_contr
ol_using_bugs?language=en Pesticides
https://www.bing.com/videos/search?q=ted+talks+garbage+island
&qpvt=ted+talks+garbage+island&FORM=VDRE Garbage Island

Other

http://geneticroulettemovie.com/
http://cotap.org/reduce-carbon-footprint/
http://www.oceanhealthindex.org/news/Death_By_Plastic
www.panna.org
https://www.caltonnutrition.com/rich-food/wallet-guide/
www.gracelinks.org